GET REAL PEOPLE

SAVE YOURSELF
CAN YOU SURVIVE

BY BILL HURLEY

"A prudent man foresees the difficulties ahead and prepares for them; the simpleton goes blindly on and suffers the consequences." -

Proverbs 22:3

"Chance favors only the prepared mind"

Louis Pasteur

INTRODUCTION

DOOMSDAY YEA RIGHT, I really do not think it is going to happen, but just in case…

I have seen the shows about all the good folks trying to prepare for doomsday, just to have the so called experts tell them they are not really prepared not enough food or water and their house or bunkers are not very good. The security plan they have, will not protect their families and what is the X factor. If you stop and think about what they are saying, you cannot really be prepared enough.

I on the other hand will try to give a few suggestions using a common sense approach, I live in the real world, and I was raised in the country and live in the city, what I have learned from research and in many cases and more importantly real life. Books and TV shows cannot replace real life. There is no one size fits all in survival or being prepared.

That being said, my planning is for two people my wife

and myself, we are planning not only to survive, we are planning to live as comfortably as possible and to be around for a long time.

You can use my planning, as a starting point, if you like. The point is, make a plan.

GET REAL PEOPLE

INDEX

GET REAL PEOPLE

CHAPTER 1

A LITTLE ABOUT ME

Allow me to tell you a little bit about myself, now don't get me wrong, I do not want you to think I am bragging about how smart I am, it is just that I learned a few things living in the country and working on farms and cotton mills, when I was much younger.

My friends and I hunted, fished, cleaned, cooked, and ate our catch. We did not catch or kill anything just for sport.

We camped out, even in the winter; we did not have fancy tents and camping gear. We would just grab an old tarp, a couple of old blankets, some rope and a couple of books of matches, strap them on our bicycles and we were good to go. If we wanted something, we worked for it, if we broke something we would fix it.

We did not have the money to take it to the repair shop, so we learned how to do for ourselves.

We did not think we were learning how to survive, we were just having fun, and man o man did we have fun.

Back then, there was always someone older and smarter, who was more than happy to teach us young whipper-snappers something new, most of the time they got a good laugh in the process.

They always love to prank us, most of the time their pranks helped us to learn not to do something again, well most of the time anyway.

Back then, we knew it all, or at least we thought we did, now many years later, I realize how dumb we were and I wish I had paid a lot more attention.

Now when I research something, many things are starting to come back to me, I must have learned more than I realized and I needed something to jump-start my memory.

I feel it is my turn to help keep the old ways alive and not just in the memories. Who knows maybe some of the old ways combined with the new technology can help me to survive for a while anyway.

Remember the saying if you don't remember the past you will repeat it, well folks repeating some of the things in the past is not a bad thing. I can only hope some of the stuff I put in here helps you out in the event that something bad happens.

I truly hope nothing does happen. If it does, I will be prepared and I hope you will be prepared as well.

Keep in mind that old saying, you can lead a horse to water but you can not make it drink.

CHAPTER 2

WHERE I LIVE

I want to tell you a little bit about where I currently live, I feel this is very important and in the following chapters it will become very clear why and how the different parts come together to help me, my wife and maybe a few others survive, for hopefully many years.

The subdivision I live in is a somewhat large subdivision with over 400 homes. There are only two entrances into the subdivision. The subdivision has a large swimming pool and a well for irrigation. Several homes have their own private swimming pool and wells also.

The entire subdivision has a network of storm drains with street inlets, yard inlets and all outlets are in the rear of the home sites. These outlets dump in to creeks or into a detention pond. Less than one half mile there is a 10 plus acre pond fed by several creeks and nice size lake fed by three rivers.

My modest brick house is at the end of a short cul-de-sac. My water supply is from public utility, I have my own septic system.

There are house on both sides, paved street in the front and best of all my back yard is very open and 150 deep, behind that are several acres of heavily wood undeveloped land.

My heating is by natural gas, natural gas vent less, fireplace and a wood burning stove. My water heater also uses natural gas to heat the water.

The house is on a crawl space foundation with 2-6 feet headroom clearance. There is a room over the two car garage, has one entry point, and one window facing the street. The attic access is through the room over there is also a window in the attic, which also faces the street.

The reason I know so much about this subdivision and my house is simple, I helped development the subdivision and designed and built my house.

I wish I could tell you this was a grand plan that came up with 20 something years ago, but that would be a big fat one; you know kinda like that beachfront property or that bridge for sale cheap. All I can say is a blind hog finds an acorn once in a while.

Not everything will work for you, be willing to try something different, tighten you belt, ask for help when you need it and give help when you can.

It is not the end of the world, only GOD can do that, and when he is ready, there is not anything you can do about it.

Therefore, until that happens all you can do is make the best of whatever situation that arises.

Remember these Words

"A prudent man foresees the difficulties ahead and prepares for them; the simpleton goes blindly on and suffers the consequences." -

Proverbs 22:3

"Chance favors only the prepared mind"

Louis Pasteur

CHAPTER 3

NETWORKING

A SELECT GROUP OF LIKE-MINDED PEOPLE

My goal is not only to survive, but also to live, to feed and protect my family and close friends by whatever means necessary.

I realized that I cannot do it alone so I have formed a network, so in the unlikely event of a natural or man made disaster they will come together with supplies, weapons and skill sets.

My network came about by accident, I was out with some friends having dinner, and someone ask had anyone watched any of those survival, or prepper shows, well we all got a good laugh, as it turned out everyone had watch the shows, and we started talking about some of the stuff we had seen and how dumb a lot of it was. I ask one person why he thought it was dumb. To my surprise, he told me he was retired military.

I already knew he could hunt, fish and cook, and I knew he was in the military what I did not know was he was an instructor at a training school. I half hearted said you could teach me survival skills, to my surprise he said he would be glad to.

That got me wondering, how many of my other friends have abilities that I was unaware that they have. I figured a good way to find out, was to ask if they had seen any of dumb shows on television and depending on their answer and reaction, I would be able determine their mind set, if they just blew it off, and changed the subject. I would not walk through the door but would leave it open and ever now and then drop a hint and wait to see what if anything would happen, maybe they were feeling me out as well.

Sometimes if I got the right reaction, I would make a statement, I think I am going to start my on network; just about everybody just laughed it off, because they thought I was kidding or just full of it. Then a strange thing started to happen, I started getting phone calls asking if I were serious about the network, then they would ask me what I would or could do to survive. After a little more talking, some of them just flat asked if they could be in my network. As the days pasted some of us started taking more about the network, and they would ask me how it was coming along.

What really surprised me was when a couple of my friends ask me to come up with a plan and to tell them what I wanted them to do; they started telling me their ideals and what they had started collecting and asking what could they do to help? I started wondering why they were asking me what to do, most all of my friend have been to college, served in the military or have been in law enforcement, just about everybody I know has more formal education and training than I do, so why me.

I asked a few of my friends why they wanted to by part of my network, why they thought I could come up with a plan that would work, their answers surprised me, they said, I do not over think things and use a common sense approach to solve problems and that I knew when to ask for help if I needed it.

I have listed some of the Skill sets that I feel should be included in any network.

> Hunter/gather/ trapper
>
> Fishing
>
> Security
>
> Farming/gardening
>
> Carpentry
>
> Energy production
>
> Medical / biological
>
> Communication
>
> Food preparation
>
> Willingness to learn

I realize that not everyone will have expertise in some of these skill sets, but may bring other skills to the network. The most important skill is that everyone does everything to help everyone. There is no one person jobs, if they can not cook the potato then they can peel it, if you don't know how to peel the potato someone will show you how to.

The bottom line is everyone must contribute to the well being of the group.

What not to bring is ego or a smarter than attitude, it has to be an all for one and one for all group. Be very, very careful who you ask to join your network, remember there may come a time when you are force to ask or even tell them to leave.

If someone has small children, how dose the parents teach and discipline their children. That is not my job and you really do not want it to be, if their child is a problem so are they.

My network consists of a small select group of like minder people. My network may include but of course, it is not limited to just these:

Doctors and Nurses
Retired and Active Military

Retired and Active Law Enforcement

Equipment Operator

Farmers

Carpenters

Electricians

Mechanics

Managers

Workers

Plumbers

Sales people

Some that just knows now to get things done

And then there is me……

What ever they do is not the most important thing; the most important thing is mutual respect for each other and their ability to work together.

Now let us look at what you might need to survive in the unlikely event something dose happen.

GET REAL PEOPLE

CHAPTER 4

WATER

The so-called experts say you can survive around 3 days without water and that you need about 3 quarts, sorry folks I is still use the American measurement system and I have no plan on changing now.

GET REAL PEOPLE. Two people need about 23 gallons per day 160 per week, 690 per month, and around 8300 gallons for just one year to live not just survive, think about it you need water to drink, you got to have water to cook, wash yourself and cloths, brush your teeth and unless you are going to do your business in the woods, you need water to flush the toilet with, provided you have your own septic system (remember chapter 2 where I live) If you are on public water and sewer and the power goes out for an extended period of time, good luck. Yes, they will turn on their generators, until fuel to runs out. You need to remember you are just not that important to them, and neither are the other tens of thousands of people all wanting the same thing.

If you think, the government will come riding in like a Knight on a white horse to save you, think again. They will be looking out for themselves. In the following pages you will see some charts with calculations and estimates, go ahead and check the math if you would like, and find all the mistakes and argue each and every point if you would like to, frankly, it is no skin off my back, because you are missing the point.

Here is the point you will be missing, if you fail to plan, you plan to fail, so waste your time trying to prove me wrong, or you can use your head and make your own plan.

I am willing to bet my life I can survive using my plan. You should also realize that any plan may need to be adjusted from time to.

Another very important thing to remember, if you try something and it does not work, try something different. Just do not give up.

GET REAL PEOPLE

When trying to determine how much water you need remember it is not just about drinking,

When trying to determine how much water you need remember it is not just about drinking,			
CHART 1 MODERATELY CONSERVATIVE 2 people			
Shower	6 minutes	1.6 gallons per min	9.6
Toilet	4 per day	1.6 gallons per	4.8
Brush teeth	4 per day	gallons per day	0.5
Drinking		gallons per day	2
cooking		gallons per day	2
dish wash			4
cloths wash			
		daily	22.9
		week	160.30
		month	689.29
		year	8271.48

CHART 2 VERY CONSERVATIVE 2 people			
Shower	6 minutes	1.6 gallons per min	9.6
teeth	4 per day	gallons per day	0.5
Drinking		gallons per day	2
cooking		gallon per day	1
dish wash			2
		daily	15.1
		week	105.70
		month	454.51
		year	5454.12
CHART 3 EXTREMELY CONSERVATIVE 2 people			
Drinking		gallons per day	2

As the chart shows in my case, we need about 23 gallons per day, 160 per week, 690 per month, or 8300 per year. It will be next to impossible to store over 8300 gallons of water, per year, it would take almost 150 fifty five gallons barrels to store that much water.

Now that you have an idea about how much water you might need, how are you going to store that much water and where are you going to get the water from?

Rain is a good place to start I have collected information from the internet to determine the average yearly and monthly rain for my area, and to be honest I was shocked to see how many gallons of rain we get in this area.

To find the amount of rain fall you get per month or year, all you need to go is search the internet.

Now is the time to do the research, if you wait it will be too late. I suggest you check several sites to confirm the information you are looking at is correct.

The saying they can not put anything on the internet if it is not true, well if you believe that you are a sandwich short of a picnic, and are dumber than a box of rocks.

I think with a little planning water is not that big of a problem, but you do need a plan. Now is the time to come up with a plan, do not wait until it something happens, it will be to late then.

It takes about 1 inch of rain to cover one square foot 1 inch deep, which equals approximately 0.62 gallon.

This chart show how much rainwater you can collect.

		1 inch rain		2 inches rain	
		gallons per square foot		gallons per square foot	
	SQFT	0.62		1.24	
	surface area	gallons collected	55 gallon barrels	gallons collected	55 gallon barrels
10x10	100	62	1	124	2
10x20	200	124	2	248	5
20x20	400	248	5	496	9
20x30	600	372	7	744	14
20x40	800	496	9	992	18
20x50	1000	620	11	1240	23
My House	2500	1550	28	3100	56

If I can collect the rain fall off the roof of my house and only average 1 inch of rain per month I should be able to collect 1550 gallons per month or 18,600 gallons per year that's over twice the water we need.

I suggest you enough storage for a month supply of water about 690 gallons, that's almost thirteen (13) 55-gallon barrels, that could be a problem, 13 barrels take up a lot of room. I found some containers called TOTES they are about four feet wide 4 feet long and four feet tall and hold about 275 gallons, I found some in the internet close to where I live for around $75 and they fit in the crawl space under my house and no ones knows they are there.

If you cannot find 55 gallon barrels or totes, you could run up to the Wal-Mart, buy a small inflatable swimming pool. The one I have is a 15 feet diameter 30-inch deep pool that holds 2800 gallons and with a cover and it cost less than $ 100.00

I figure we need 2 gallons of drinking water per day or around 62 gallons per month. I currently have about a one-month supply, which is, about twelve cases of ready to drink water on hand.

128 OUNCES = 1 GALLON					
case	bottles	oz per bottle	total oz	oz per gal	gallons
1	40	16.9	676	128	5.3
5	200	16.9	3380	128	26.4
10	400	16.9	6760	128	52.8
12	480	16.9	8112	128	63.4

I have been drinking bottled water for some time now and realized that I have been throwing away storage containers, so I started saving the empty bottles so I can refill them and store even more water. I save all plastic bottles and jugs to store water, and food stuffs.

I recommend you purify any water that has been stored for and extended period of time before you drink it. I made a rack using scrap plywood and cutting holes the size of the bottles

I rotate the older bottles with new ones. Stock rotation is always a good idea with any consumable items.

I have over 1000 gallons of additional water, so without doing anything I have over a one month supply of water this will allow me time to set up my collection system.

If I need to, I can make water runs to the wells, swimming pools, ponds or the lake. You need to remember water weights about 8 pounds per gallon. Hauling large amounts of water will be hard.

I have several 15 gallon barrels, several 5 gallon buckets and a four wheeled wagon that will hold two of the 15 gallon barrels or around 30 gallons 4 five gallon buckets. That still is going to way 200 to 300 pounds when you include the water, wagon and barrels, that is more than one person can handle, so wait until a couple of your network people get there then make the run to collect water from the other source you are located.

I don't suggest you drink unpurified rain water or any unpurified water for that matter, remember the swimming pool, ponds and the lake that I mentioned earlier, you had better purify this ware if you plan to use it.

I am not going to leave you hanging, after doing a lot of research, I have just ordered what it think is the best water purifier on the market. The Berkey Water Filters come in several different sizes, and prices and their website have a lot good information as well.

I decided to get one, if for no other reason is just to have better drinking water on a daily bases, I got a couple of extra filters, you know just in case. Here is a tip for you keep a gallon of bleach on hand. It will come in handy.

There are many different styles and brands of filters on the market. This is not where you want to cut corners. That could be a mistake you cannot live with. If all your filters and purifiers stop working you, can always make yourself a distiller or sometimes known as a still.

They are really easy to make, just take a big metal pot, put a lid on the pot you need to drill a hole in the lid, so you can connect a vent pipe which is also your condensing coil, fill it with water. Build a fire under it. When the water boils, it turns to steam that goes out the vent pipe or condensing coil, which cools the steam turning it back in to pure distilled water.

Sounds simple don't it, well folks if you don't know what you are doing you could be making a very powerful bomb, if it builds up to much pressure it can and will explode.

I recently purchased a used stainless steel beer keg.

I removed the tap spout, and replace it with removable stainless steel nipple and T joint. On one end of the T, I added another short nipple and a cutoff valve I will use this to refill the keg with unpurified water. On the other end of the T fitting, I add my condensing coil. For extra safety, I also added a pressure relief valve. I prefer stainless steel but copper and brass will work and maybe cheaper and easier to find at the hardware store.

You can use propane to boil the water until it runs out then you can burn wood, either you need to make a rack to set it on, the rack needs to fairly strong the keg holds about 15 gallons of water so when it is full it will weigh over 100 pounds. A couple of cement blocks will make an inexpensive stand and can be used as a grill stand as well.

I suggest filtering the water first to get the big stuff out, a window screen will do the trick, and I will add eight drops of bleach to each gallon.

People if you are in this situation where you need to filter your water you can not be to careful now is not the time to get a stomach bug, it could kill you or make you wish you were dead.

Drawing 1 below shows the basic set up, On the second drawing I added a cooling tank, it is not necessary but there are 2 reasons I added the cooling tank, the first is simple it will cool the steam down faster. The second is just an added benefit warm water to use for cleaning and bathing. As the steam, flows through the coil the water in the cooling tank draw the heat out of the steam turning the steam back into water, which heats the water in the cooling tank. If you need to you can reused the water from the cooling tank.

You might be able to use this system to distill alcohol for fuel, I have not tried it for that and will not, that would be illegal and will get you put in jail. If you want to take the risk and try to make fuel alcohol I would not try to drink it might kill you.

I plan to use my keg still ONLY as a backup to make clean safe drinking water. Yes, you can laugh at my drawings, but the system works and can be built for around $100.

I use a keg because I had one, you make a distiller out of a lot of different things, like a pressure cooker, even a metal trash can, yep that works also.

My Keg Still

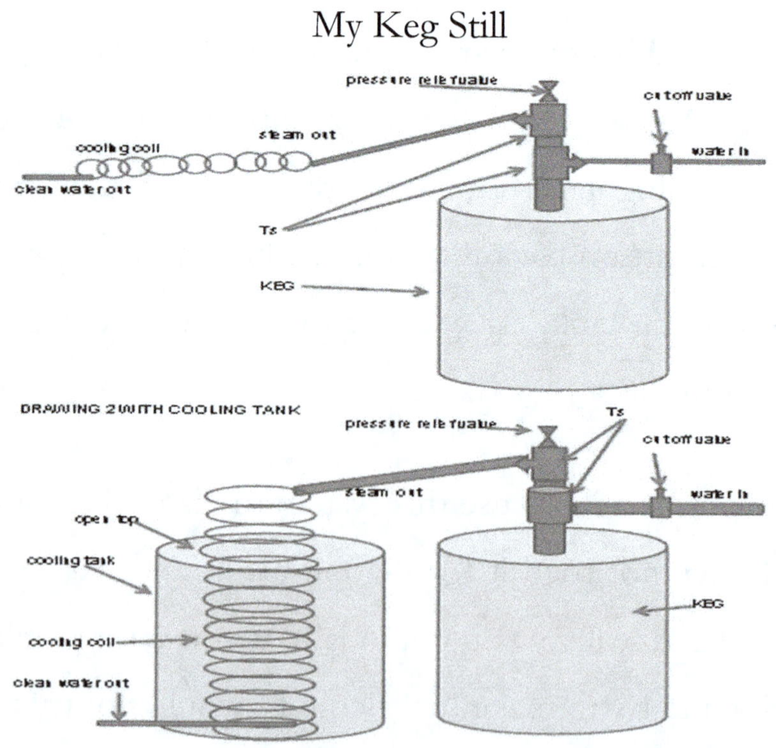

You can buy a water distiller from many different places, I just decided to see if I could make one, I did and it works.

I have mapped out all the swimming pools, houses that have wells and the routes to take to get to them.

On a different map I mapped out the routes to the ponds and lakes with multiple access points to get water from them.

Having clean water is just not a problem if you have a plan.

Just remember the saying; if you fail to plan, you plan to fail.

CHAPTER 5

FOOD and COOKING

Below are items. Everyone should bring with them. Everyone needs to understand that once anything enters the location, the group will share it, the only exception is personal life sustaining medicines.

They need to bring pretty much everything that does not require refrigeration. We may have a generator for a time, which means we may be able to refrigerate for a short time or at least until the normal fuel runs out and maybe even after when normal fuel runs out.

RICE

Rice is a cheap food source I bought 50 pounds at Sam's club for less than $18. We eat rice anyway so even if nothing happens it will not go to waste, Rice will keep a very long time; just keep it in a cool airtight place away from moister and light. I used my food saver vacuum sealer to make bags that hold 2 cups, the amount we normally use for a meal; you can make a lot of different things with rice.

CORN

Corns, again very inexpensive, go to the feed store that's right, feed store you know the place that sales feed for live stock horses, cows, 50 pounds cost around $12, you can make all sorts of thing with corn, corn also keeps a long time again just keep it in a cool air tight place away from moister and light

BEANS

There are many types of dried bean, pinto, Lima, black-eyed peas, green peas, butter beans white beans, navy beans. I think you get my point, dried bean do not cost a lot are high in protein and are very easy to prepare, you can mix different types bean and as I showed you earlier water is not a problem you can even make soup. I know I said this before, but it is important to remember, beans will keep a long time again. Just keep them in a cool airtight place away from moister and light.

SUGAR

You can live with out sugar, but it does make life sweeter and a little goes a long way. You may need sugar for other things as well alcohol comes to mind.

YEAST

Yeast is handy to have around, it can help when you when you want to bake thing or make a treat like rice pudding. Remember the corn, sugar and the keg still, I am just saying…

ALCOHOL

Disinfectant or use as a fuel source. You might be able to sale it or trade it for something else you may need or GET REAL PEOPLE have some fun.

SALT

You cannot live with out salt. Salt makes food taste better. You can use salt as a preservative, in years gone by people use to cure meat and fish using salt. Salt is cheap, and will keep forever, just keep it dry. If you live near the ocean, you can use the keg still to get fresh water and salt.

Yep my keg still is starting make since now.

SPICES, HERBS, and SEASONINGS

These add flavor to foods and some have added health benefits. I may grow some, but will buy most of what I think I will need.

I know the dried herbs are not as good as fresh, but if you are in this situation, where are you going to get fresh, you may be able grow some herbs, and dehydrate them for future use, if you have time to wait.

I buy the big bottle/jars, it is easier to buy them, and they are not that expensive. They will stay good for a long time; just keep the containers dry and sealed.

Below are a few of my got to haves:

Garlic power and salt

Dried dice onions

Ginger

Parsley

Basil

Chili powder

Black pepper ground and corns

Cheyenne pepper

Celery seed

Oregano

Cilantro

Cinnamon

Beef bullion granular

Chicken bulling granular

Salt

GROWING and SEEDS

You had better figure this out or you will not survive; you cannot store enough food to last forever.

Before you think about planting a garden you need to think about what you are going to plant and when to plant it, how much water do you need, what kind of fertilizer do you need and where are you going to get it. Therefore, you can see it not as easy as it sounds. Something you should consider is yield per square foot, does your garden get enough sunlight and how do you keep critters out of your garden, rabbits birds, squirrels deer and turtles love fresh vegetables just as much as you do.

DO NOT BUY HYBRID SEEDS, they will grow and yes you can eat the harvest, but the seed from your harvest will not grow, so you need seeds to plant, that produce planting seeds also.

A few things that may help are:

Fencing
I suggest using chicken wire. Chicken wire is kind of like a net and will keep most critters out, and depending on the size of your garden; you may be able to cover the top to keep birds out.

Cans and pie plates
Surround your garden with string, wire, or rope, if you are using cans put some rocks in the cans and tie the cans on the a string or wire, if something hits the string it will cause the rocks in the can to rattle, and scare the critter, this works for bigger critters. Do the same thing

with the pie plates with out the rocks, when the wind blows the pie plate will bang against something it will also reflect light scaring critters off.

One critter that will be harder to protect your garden from is the two-legged kind, on this one let your conscience be your guide.

HUNTING

Hunting is a good way to increase your food supply, small game, birds, rabbits and squirrels are somewhat plentiful in my area, but the more people hunting them. the supply will become harder to find and shoot. I suggest using a 22 rifle; it will do less damage to your game and make less noise than a high caliber weapon or a shotgun.

The small size of these animals will supply food for a couple of people without wasting food. The part you cannot eat can be used, for a few other things like bait for trapping and fishing and fertilizer for growing food. Remember what the Indians and Pilgrims did year ago.

GET REAL PEOPLE

If you decide to hunt large game, like deer, wild hogs and well, let us just say things you would not ever think about eating but GET REAL PEOPLE. If you get really Hungry, you will eat things you would not have thought you would eat., you should use a large caliber weapon, rifle, shotgun, if using a shotgun use buckshot or slugs if you use a smaller shot it could just wound the animal it would just run off and die later and you have wasted food.

A problem with larger game is there will be more than you can eat without it going bad, having a network in place is good for a lot of reasons, share the larger game with them, and they should do the same with you. Another option is to smoke, cure, and dehydrate the meat, do not forget the salt. I said you could not live without.

It is a good ideal to cook all the meat as soon as you can, cooked meat keeps longer than uncooked meat. You can also sale and trade meat, but before you let it go bad give it to someone, you never know they might remember you helped them and they might help you at some point. You can always use help cutting and gathering wood to use for heating, cooking, and smoking meat and fish.

FISHING

Fishing, if you have access to lakes and ponds have some fishing hooks, you can catch fish. When you are digging your garden pay attention to the worms and other bug you dig up they make good fish bait and if you have a pile of old leafs rake them back you mostly will find some bait there as well and remember the part of the animals you could not eat, yep more bait to fish with.

Do not get greedy, catch only enough to eat, unless you are planning to, smoking or salt curing them, if you are, they will last a longer time. If your fish were to go bad remember you can to use them for bait to catch more fish or for fertilizer in you garden like the Native Americans showed the pilgrims to do.

DEHYDRATOR

Dehydrating food is a good way to preserve all kinds of food. I have an electric dehydrator I use quite often to make jerky, don't ask me how long my jerky will keep, because it taste so good we eat it up in a couple of weeks, I just made a batch using very lean ground beef, it will be gone in 2 weeks.

You most likely will not have refrigeration so you need a dehydrator and since you mostly will not have electricity, you need to a make or buy a dehydrator.

If you have a barbeque grill, you have a dehydrator and a smoker. Low heat for along time is the key, meat only need to get to 165 degrees for six to eight hours to be smoked or dehydrated, You should cut it to 1/8 to 1/4 inch thick, the thicker the meat the longer it takes in the case longer is better.

You may have heard of a smoke house, well in days gone by, that is how people would preserve meat; they could smoke enough meat to last all year long. You can also, dry fruit, vegetables, and fish. It will take a lot less time to dry these, be careful not over dry, you can still eat them if you do they just will not be as good. Be very, very careful not to under dry any kind of meat, under dried meat can make you sick or even kill you.

CANNING

Yep just, like your Grandma use to do. You had better learn to do it right or it could kill you or at least make you so sick you would wish you were dead.

There are two ways to can food. The first is a hot water bath and this is where you put you jars and product with the lids on, in a pot of boiling water for a period different. Thing require different times.

After the jars and product have cooked long enough, turn the heat off and let cool down. The cooling will cause a vacuum to be created in the jar sealing the lid to the jar, if the lid is pulled down in the center it is sealed sometimes you may hear a pop, this is a good thing, that is just the lid being pulled down. This method is good for most vegetables or as they say low acid foods, but not meat.

The other way and most likely the safest way is pressure cooker canning. I used to think by boiling something it would kill germs and bacteria, well as it turn out that is not very true. Botulism will not be killed until the temperature reaches 240 degrees, ok if water boils at 212 degrees how do you get the temperature to 240 degrees Yes, I had to ask someone, by putting water under pressure, 15 psi or more the temperature of the water can reach 240 degrees which will kill botulism and that is why you need a pressure cooker.

Both are done in the same way one is without pressure the other one uses pressure.

You need to pay attention and be extra careful when using a pressure cooker.

Canned food can last a long time, but you notice the lid pushed up throw it away, it lost its seal, and that is not good.

You can get a lot of information on canning and a good pressure cooker from Presto.com.

That is the kind my mother and grandma used and I bought a sixteen-quart model for myself. The sixteen is the size of the pot not how quart jars you can prepare at one time, the pot will only hold 7 quart jars.

Please be very carful when using a pressure cooker, make sure it is in better than good working condition. Anytime you put something under high pressure without a proper relief valve it could build up so much pressure and EXPLODE.

CHAPTER 6

HEALTH and HYGIENE

FIRST, OF ALL I AM NOT A DOCTOR AND ONLY A REAL DOCTOR CAN AND SHOULD give MEDICAL ADVICE SO PLEASE TALK WITH YOU DOCTOR BEFORE YOU TRY ANY HOME REMEDIES, AND LISTEN TO WHAT THEY TELL YOU.

MEDICINES

Medicines will be difficult to stock up on making it hard for some people to survive for an extended period. It may sound crazy but when in survival mode you may benefit, since food will be limited, you could lose weight. The day to day grind of your lifestyle will change, hopeful making things less stressful and as they tell you, eat better, lose weight, reducing you stress could relieve a lot of you health problems.

VITAMINS

Get a good supply of multi vitamins with minerals. One a day per person, make sure they have lots of Vitamin C.

I am planning for 2 years for two people so I will have 365 x 2 = 730 per year or 1460 for 2 years. I do not care how good your food supply is you will need to take your vitamins.

FIRST AID KIT

Buy a big, well stock first aid kit. It should have things to treat minor cut and scraps, rashes like poison oak and ivy, bee stings, bug bites. Make sure the kit has rubbing alcohol, peroxide, and antibiotic cream and antiseptic spray. Cream would be a better choice, it is less wasteful.

In your kit, add a surgical kit one the can be use to sew up more serious cuts, stop right there big boy unless you know what you are doing, don't try this at home, unless you can not find a doctor, nurse or someone trained to do this.

There are other things that can be used to close a

wound, butterflies, I not talking about the bug, there is some kinds of adhesive strips that is also used. There is a liquid adhesive that can be used to glue a small cut together.

You need to think about the pain associated with being sewed and what about infection. You could maybe get some Betadine that will last for a while, then what ya gonna do, well that's easy, remember my keg still, you can make 190 proof alcohol which will kill germs and brain cells, it may not stop the pain, but at least you want care if you drink enough.

It has been said that I have a horse shoe up my rear end, and I think that may be true, I am married to a nurse, several of my other friends are nurses, have first aid training, or in some way are in the medical field and get this doctors.

If you are not as lucky as I am, you may know some one who is qualified to help when and if you need it. You need to remember everyone may have something or some service that that could help each other and if you have planned well enough, you may have something to trade.

ASPIRIN

I know some people cannot take aspirin, then get what you can take, Tylenol, Advil the point is it is a pain reliever can reduce a fever.

ALLERGY RELIEF

I like Sudafed, it works for me. The only problem with Sudafed is that you now have to sign for it at the drug store. I am not planning to do illegal things with it; it is just a pain in the rear end to have to sign for.

There are many products on the market; I suggest you get what works for you.

DUST MASK

Get the good ones, but any will help when the pollen is in the air, which seems like all the time anymore. Dust mask could offer some protection from other more dangerous thing as well. Do not go the cheap route; be sure to get some good ones.

DENTAL WAX

Dental wax is a great quick temporary fix. If you get a tooth, ache, just soften the wax, and by kneading it with your fingers, then place it over the affected tooth. It helps keep the air off the nerve, reducing the amount pain.

SPLINTS, ACE BANDAGES AND TAPE

These are a got to have type thing, in case someone breaks a bone. Cheap and easy to find and a splint can be a board or a limb out of a tree. You can also make a crutch using a tree limb.

You should be thinking about what you need and plan for it, you are the best person to decide what is right for you not me.

I do not think I need to go into many details here or at least I hope I do not, getting sick on injured will not be much fun,

Hygiene is a very important part to good health. I will also list some thing that you should plan to have

DEODORANTS

Stick or roll on are better for long-term use. The human body needs to sweat. Sweating is the way the body regulates body temperature and keeps you from over heating. You just do not need to stink while you are sweating.

BIODEGRADABLE SOAP

One that is antibacterial is the best choice. I like Dawn, it is also a good grease remover as well.

SHAMPOO

Your choice, if you can use the same soap that you use to wash your body it would be better, because you don't need to have so many different products. It is far more important to be clean than to look pretty. Shampoo will not be something I will worry about, because I will shave my head, of course, my wife will probably want to kill me, but she will get over it, or at least I hope she will.

TOOTH BUSH AND PASTE

Any is better than not having any at all. Toothpaste may help you from getting a toothache and your friends you thank you for not have bad breath

BAKING SODA

Baking soda can be used for many things including toothpaste and heartburn relief. Baking soda can also be used as a cleaning agent. Do not confuse baking powder with baking soda they are to very different things and react differently with other stuff.

HAND SANITIZERS

You can by large bottles of hand sanitizers, and it is not that expensive. Use hand sanitizer before you handle any food product, that way you do not contaminate the rest of your food or may some one else sick.

Plain old water is a hand sanitizer. Washing yours hands with water will help if nothing else available.

TOILET PAPER

Don't forget the TP, I bought 4 cases of Georgia Pacific

- Envision, Recycled Bath Tissue, 2-Ply, 550 Sheets - 80 Rolls from Sam's Club about $46 a case should last a couple of years.

When that runs out you can always use old newspapers, books, magazines, old rages, and do not forget phones books. Do not use the slick glossy pages, you will figure out why. It helps if you crumple it up real good, which will make it a little softer, also if soak it in water for a short time, let it dry, then crumple it up it will be even softer.

A roll of TP has several hundred sheets a large phone book has a thousand. I think you get my point here.

Most people will not think about this but it is so very important.

Just remember good hygiene make for good health and will help you keep your friends.

It might sound crazy but having a sick room is not a bad

idea. It will be very easy to make one using plastic, just pick a room and cover the doorway with plastic. If someone needs to enter the sick room, they should always wear a mask, it might need them from getting sick as well. If you can take a small fan and place it in a window blowing outside, it will help remove germs and could pull cleaner air into the room.

If you can, wear gloves when you are trying to help a sick friend and always wash your hands when you leave the room, you do not want to get your other friend sick do you.

Use some common sense when it comes to health and hygiene. You should have been taught, about health and hygiene all your life and now is the time to remember what you were taught, proper hygiene can same your life.

CHAPTER 7

TOOLS

Tools will be very important in you effort to survive. Most of the things I have listed below are thing I have had for years and there is a good chance you may have many of these tools as well. The things I did not have I have purchased or in some cases made.

FARADAY CAGE

I sounds like this would be hard to find or difficult to may, but is so easy even I could do it and I did. My small one is made using a Behrens 31 gallon. Steel Trash Can I bought at Home depot.

I bought a couple of cans of flex seal, you know the stuff they advertise on TV, where the cut a opening in the bottom of a boat and then attach a screen door over the opening then spray it with flex seal, put in water and it floats and does not leak. I do not know about the boat part, but I do this is good stuff and it can may a watertight seal.

Spray the inside of the trashcan, sides and bottom, do not be skimpy with it either. The can comes with a lid. PAY ATTENTION HERE, take piece of painter's tape, blue or green it does not matter, you can even duct tape if you have it, painter's tape is just easier to remove.

Tape the flange, lip, the part that will slide down over the outside of the can, around the entire lid, this is done so you don't get the flex seal on the flange. Now spray bottom of the lid, when everything is dry remove the tape, you do this so you have a metal to metal connection with the lid and the can thus allowing the EMP to flow around the can and not in it.

Two simple tests are, take battery operated radio turn it on place it in the can put the lid on tight, if you no longer hear the radio play it is working. The other test in a dark room or at night place a bright flashlight in the can look all around the lid of the can if you do not see light it is working. If you do see light, mark the spot, remove the lid, spray some more flex seal in the area, let dry and repeat until you see no light.

Place your electronics inside the can, if you can put them in a zip lock type bag, which would be even better. The zip lock bag will help keep moisture and water out. Wrap them with newspaper this is an extra layer of protection, newspaper is made from wood and wood does not conduct electricity.

I suggest using some bungee cords to hold the lid I place. You should place the can on bare ground and if you can drive a copper ground rod in to the ground take a piece of copper wire connect the can to the ground rod.

You should you should keep the can in as cool place and never in direct sun light it will act like a oven and could melt you electronics.

It cost me about $30 dollars to make this FARADAY CAGE and it can be used as a water storage container that holds 31 gallons.

The trash can FARADAY CAGE is a good way to protect you small stuff, but if you have larger thing like a generator, or solar panels or anything that will fit into a trash then you can build one.

It is easy and not that expensive to build a large FARADAY CAGE or even a room. Build a frame using 2x4s cover all for sides and the top and

Bottom with plywood or OSB/wafer board. Once you have your box put together rap all sides, top and bottom with aluminum roof flashing that you can get at most hardware stores. Be sure to have at least a 2 inch overlap on all seams, attach with aluminum roofing nails or staples make sure the nails or staples DO NOT penetrate the inside of the box. When you add your door, cut the hole in the box, attach your hinges and latch over the flashing. It is important that you cover the gap between the door and the box again with flashing.

I suggest doing this with screws and again DO NOT penetrate the inside of the box. For added protection, spray the inside of the box with flex seal. You should test it the same way you tested the cage.

DUCT TAPE

Hundreds maybe thousand of uses and you cannot have to enough duct tape. If you do not have several rolls of duct tape, go buy them.

AXE

Cutting wood and can be use as a weapon, get one that has the cutting edge on just one side, the other side can be used as a hammer.

HATCHET

Chopping small wood for kindling and can also be used for butchering food. It can also be use as a weapon.

MACHETE

Machetes are great cutting small stuff. It can also be use as a weapon.

HAND SAWS

For cutting boards, and firewood.

CROSSCUT SAW

When you run out of gas, use the crosscut saw to cut

down bigger trees for firewood. I was surprised that crosscut saws are still being made, and price $75 and up.

HACK SAW

You need a hacksaw to cut metal and bones in the game you have hunted, I think you see why you need a hacksaw.

SHOVELS

Round point shovels are for digging and square head shovels for moving material.

MADDOX

Get one that has a digger on one side and blade on the other for cutting roots and wood in a pinch.

MULTI TOOLS

Multi tools are easy to carry and a must have; pliers, knife, can opener, and screwdrivers all in one kit. I think it would be a good idea to have several on hand, they always come in handy, and they are not very expensive either. Carry one with you wherever you go you never know when you might need a multi tool.

ROPE

Use to secure things, and yes if need be people, also use to attach to well bucket to draw water from wells. A good nylon rope is better, stronger and will last longer.

FISHING LINE and HOOKS

Of course use for fishing, can also be used to make booby traps

LEATHER, RUBBER & LATEX GLOVES

I think you know what to do with theses, or at least I hope you do because if you do not know what to do with them, you are dumber than a box of rocks.

TOOLS and TOOL BOX

Adjustable wench, pipe wrench, vise grips, pliers regular and channel lock, and all kinds of screw drives. If you wear, glasses get an eyes glass repair it.

HAND AIR PUMP

Inflate tires and air masteries. No electricity and batteries needed. Just good old fashion elbow grease.

HAND WATER PUMP

Da; to pump water when you do not have electricity. A hand pump will help get water out of you storage barrels.

ON DEMAND WATER PUMP 12 VOLT

Great little pump, when you open valve water will automatically flow from you water storage tank. You will not get a lot of water fast it will have some pressure and you do not have to carry water.

HAND FUEL PUMP

Most fuels have a corrosive property which could damage a water pump, and you do want not to drink water from a pump that has been use to pump fuel.

FUEL PUMP 12 VOLT

You might find a fuel tank with some fuel left in it go ahead a borrow it I am sure the owner want mind, if they are not coming back, or they may need some help getting it out of the tank, and reward you for your help.

POLY CLEAR and BLACK

Among other things, use the clear to cover windows to

make them airtight. Attach to windows and doors using duct tape or staples.

The black poly should also be used to cover windows and doors to prevent lights from being seen especially at night.

You can also use poly to catch rain water, poly also will prevent weeds from growing in your garden and will help water your plants, water will condense under poly when place in the sun.

STEEL WOOL

Unbelievably steel wool burns, use steel wool and a battery to help start a fire.

COTTON BALLS

That's right cotton balls they are very light and make great tinder to start fire, even better if you stuff then in a piece of PVC pipe and pour some flammable liquid over them just enough to dampen the cotton balls. Use screw on caps with the PVC pipe so you will be able to remove and replace it as needed. Cotton balls are very cheap, light, and easy to store.

PVC PIPE AND FITTING

PVC pipe can be use for more than just water pipe. It makes great storage containers, for all sorts of thing, food, water, guns, ammo, and valuables.

I suggest you use a screw on fitting so you can remove the contents with out breaking the pipe and you will be able to reuse the pipe. Properly seal pipe is air and water tight, which means you can bury it under ground and have a backup supply, of food, water, guns and ammo or anything you want to keep safe.

RASP

A rasp is a very course file used to shave wood. The reason I suggest you have a rasp is so you can make course powdery wood to use a tender when building a fire. Using the rasp on fat lighter works great if you are using a bow drill to start a fire.

METAL FILE

You need to a metal file to keep your cutting tools shape.

If you have ever tried to cut something with a dull tool, you know what I mean. I suggest getting several files, both course and fine teeth.

GRAIN PRESS

Something you may want to consider getting is a small grain press. Extracting oils from grain is not the only reason to have on. You can extract the oil from fat lighter and use it in lanterns or soak a rag in the oil to make a torch.

A grain press works by adding your material to a chamber; if you heat the chamber just a little, it will make it easier to extract the oils. Simply by tightening the press it will slowly squeeze the oil out, you will not get a lot of oil at one time, but you will get some oil.

After you have extracted all the oil out, you can use the material left in the press for kindling, or if you have pressed grains, you can use that by-product to eat or feed your livestock like chickens.

If you are like me and prefer to make things, you can make a press like the one I did. I took a piece of four-inch steel pipe about a foot long, treaded on both ends.

On one end I screwed on a cap, on the cap, I drilled several small holes; I did this so the liquid could come so I could collect it.

On the other end cap, I drilled a ¾-inch hole in the center; I then welded a ¾-inch nut over the hole.

You need to get a 8 to 10 inch long treaded bolt with a hex head on it, this is needed because this is what you will turn to make the compression.

Now comes the hard part, you need to find or make a plug that fits firmly on the inside of your pipe. The plug needs to be at least ½ inch thick, and thicker is better, so the plug will not warp, if it does warp you will loose compression and the liquid will collect on the top of the plug.

Find the center of the plug, and center another plug ¾

inch over the center point, here is a little trick, when you have the nut centered in place out a few drops of super glue on the nut and plug, this will hold the nut in place so it will not move when you weld it.

Take a piece of fine mesh screen and place it in the cap with the small holes in it, now screw that cap onto the pipe, hand tight only.

Fill the pipe with the material you are going to extract the oil from, now put the other cap on, hand tight only, you are ready to start pressing. Using a wrench, turn the bolt until you can turn it any more, well at least for now.

As the oil comes out the bottom some compression will be lost, retighten the bolt, you will need to repeat the process several times. When you cannot tighten the bolt anymore and when there is no more coming out, loosen the bolt and remove the caps, when you clean the material out of the pipe save it to use latter.

CHAPTER 8

ENERGY and FUEL

SOLAR

Solar cells are becoming less expensive and are providing more power per square foot. I suggest enough panel wattage to keep a couple of deep cycle batteries charged.

WATER

If you have a steam with good running water, you can adapt a wind turbine to work with water.

INVERTER

Get an inverter with 1500 -2000 watts is large enough to run a small refrigerator. An inverter converts DC volts to AC volts, most things your house run on AC volts

RECHARGEABLE BATTERIES AND CHARGER

Rechargeable can be expensive especially if you have to buy many different sizes. I suggest you start changing the things that need batteries to ones that use the same size batteries.

GENERATORS

Generators can be very expensive to operate.

With cost of fuel and most likely no fuel, a good suggestion would be to get a tri fuel generator one that will run off of gasoline, propane, and natural.

This upgrade will cost you a couple hundred dollars more but give you a better of have fuel for a longer time a 2000-3000 watt generator will most things in your house just not all at once.

HAND AND PEDAL GENERATORS

You crank this just small generator with you hands or feet. The once I have seen so far are 300- 400 watts. They are also good for exercise as well.

WIND GENERATORS

A wind turbine generator is a good back up to help keep your batteries charged. I have seen home wind turbines from 400-600 watts.

GASOLINE, NATURAL, GAS PROPANE, AND OIL

All are expensive and good while they last.

ALCOHOL

A lot of uses and fuel is one of them, (think Keg Still), you will see why a little later.

WOOD

Look around there is wood everywhere. You can use wood for heating, cooking, lighting; you can even use wood as a weapon. Wood is one of the cheapest and easiest fuel sources you can find.

When you walk through the woods, trying to gather some firewood you also be on the lookout for lighter stumps, sometimes called fatwood, fat lighter, lighter knots or kindling. What you are looking for is old dead pine tree stump or even a log. When you think you have found one, here a quick test; kick or knock any remaining bark off the stump or log, if you find a really hard center, it could be a lighter stump, now take your axe, machete and try to cut a piece off of the stump. It should be very hard, so it is more like chipping apiece off.

Now that that you have the piece chipped off, look at the chip, it should be kind of a dark brown reddish color now smell the chip it should have a strong smell of turpentine if the chip has that it is most likely a lighter stump.

What you have is a stump that has a high concentration of flammable sap, which has dried over the years.

The last test is to set fire to the chip, it should catch fire pretty fast and give off a thick black smoke, if it does you have found what yare looking for.

Fat lighter is good for helping to start fires and if you do not have wood, it can be your firewood. The oil you will get by using a press can be used not only as a fuel, you can make a lot of thing like soap and it smells good.

There are other things you can make with the oil, but you need to research that for yourself, they are somewhat dangerous.

LIGHTING

I have been changing my light bulbs from incandescent to CFL compact Florissant blubs several years and now I have started adding LED blubs to the mix. LED light last a long time put off a bright light. LED light require a lot less electricity. The price of the LED light is getting cheaper everyday.

FLASH LIGHTS

Led flashlight are the way to go now a days, if you shop around you can get some really great deals, a few days ago at Home Depot I found a package of eight LED flashlights with batteries for $5. I did not need them, but at that price, I had to get a pack.

LANTERNS PROPANE, OIL, and GAS

The old fashion oil lanterns are still a good way to light up a room; they will give light for many hours on just little fuel.

I have couple of propane lanterns that I used when we had power outages, they use the little cans, which will last for few hours, I also have multi port adapter that allows me to connect several lanterns or stoves to a larger propane tank. Keep this in mind, you will understand later in the book.

Gas lanterns, like the one Coleman make, the ones you put unleaded gasoline, (sometime call white gas) in and pump up, it is a great lantern to have until you run out of gas, you will be happy.

There is another lantern, commonly called a Miner's light, or caver's light. It is, an Acetylene lantern, which operates by adding a very small amount of water to carbide, this produces Acetylene gas. The flame is reflected outward. Not great light, but would be nice to have. If you can find one.

I would not recommend using any lantern that burns fuel in a room that does not have good ventilation.

CANDLES

I never knew there were some many different kinds of candles, there are even some that burn for over 10 hours

I found several long burning candles on these websites, beprepared.com, and budk.com and they have a lot of other good stuff, you make want to check them out.

The Clear Mist 100 Hour Plus Emergency Candle works more like a lantern than a candle, but it last for 100 hours who cares what it looks.

MATCHES

Matches will make it so much easier to start afire, they are one of the cheapest things you can buy, so get a lot of them. It is very important to keep your matches dry.

If you can find what we use to call kitchen matches or strike anywhere matches, the ones with the white head on it, buy a good supply of them. As the name says the will strike just about anywhere, just remember do not let them get wet.

Any time I go to a restaurant of store and it has free matches, I grab a few packs

BUTANE LIGHTERS

Butane lighters or cigarettes lighters are cheap and will last a long time, if you use them to light candles and fires.

I have included a power system that would make life easier, yes, it does have a gas generator. In addition, an adapter will allow you to run it on gas, propane, or natural gas.

NPower™ Complete Solar Power Package with Backup Generator — 1800 Watts in Bypass Mode + 2200 Additional Generator Watts. I am going to add a wind turbine generator to my power system, the more option you have the better your chances are.

Sunforce Wind Generator Turbine 600 Watts

I am contacting this company to see if I can get the power head with out the blades and tail fin, I want to connect the power head to a bicycle. We all will need to get some exercise and, this would be a good way to get exercise and generate some power at the same time.

Remember back in chapter 5 when I said you'll be able to refrigerate for a short time or at least until the normal fuel runs out and maybe even when normal fuel runs out. Now you will find out what I meant by that.

Solar Refrigerator DC refrigerators can be ran on solar, wind, hydro, or battery systems.

Sundanzer Solar-Powered Chest Freezer — 8 Cubic Ft., 30in.L x 50in.W x 37in.H
Item# 121102

Sundanzer Solar-Powered Refrigerator — 8 Cubic Ft., 30in.L x 50in.W x 37in.H   Item # 121105

You maybe wondering why I have two of the same things here, look closer, one is a freezer the other is a refrigerator.

I found these at Northern Tool and Supply. Northern Tool has all sorts of great stuff that will come in handy. I call it my big boy store

CHAPTER 9

COMMUNICATION

HAND CRANK LIGHT RADIOS

I have a couple of these, the ones I have are battery, hand crank and solar and the radios are AM, FM, Short Wave and Weather all in one nice neat little package. The solar also charges the batteries.

Ambient Weather WR-111B Emergency Solar Hand Crank AM/FM/NOAA Digital Radio, Flashlight, Cell Phone Charger with NOAA Certified Weather Alert & Cables

CB RADIOS

That's right good buddy, a CB radio like we used in the 70s is still a good way to communicate there a good for short to medium long range and you can use the old 10 codes like 10-4 or 10-20. Another good to have is tell you network at what time you will be on what channel, it can be simple like at one o-clock I will monitor channel one or a little harder at one o-clock, I will monitor channel time plus 3 which mean channel 4. I think you get the point by adding a code it will be harder for unwanted people hearing what you are saying. I also suggest never using channel 9 or 19.

Channel 9 is monitored by law enforcement. Channel 19 is the most commonly used channel.

I have a couple of portable units and a mobile unit that I can use in my car or take in the house and use like a base station.

TWO WAY RADIOS

These are different from CBs and Family Radio Service (FRS) are for short range and have fewer channels, tell your network to get a set and tell them you channel.

HAM RADIOS

If you really want to reach out and touch, get a ham radio, they are rather expense and require a license to operate. You can literally talk around the world.

LASER

Good for fairly long range signaling, hard to see where it is coming from but when the beam hit the target the red dot is easy to see. When used with a code, a good choice to communicate with. Do not get a green laser the beam emitted from a green laser is visible, which will allow someone to trace it back to its source.

MIRROR

Only good in bright sun light

FLASH LIGHTS

Not a great choice because everybody can see where you are and can notice your location and code. It is hard to see in sunlight as well. If that is, all you got use it.

WHISTLES

At best, you can get someone's attention and then, they can look for another code source.

CODES

Codes are a good way to protect yourself, different type

codes for different sources is also a good thing, certain blast form a whistle, number of flashes from a light source of course verbal codes, name and transmission time, all of these could help protect you from unwanted listeners and visitors.

There so many ways to communicate it is not funny, but one of the most important is YOUR MOUTH, not just for warning or signaling, but for talking to one another, it is far better to talk to people than to allow a problem to fester until it gets out of control and starts to tear your network apart.

If you have a problem talk about, if someone else has a problem listen to them and then work it out.

Do not be stupid if you do not understand, something ask them to explain it to help you understand.

If they have a suggestion at least listen, their idea may make things easier.

If the politicians would pay attention to the

UNITED STATES CONSTITUTION

Which starts with?

We the People of the United States, in Order to form a more perfect Union, establish Justice, insure domestic Tranquility, provide for the common defence, promote the general Welfare, and secure the Blessings of Liberty to ourselves and our Posterity, do ordain and establish this for the United States of America.

If they would read and understand those words, maybe we and the world would not be in such a mess.

This can and should apply to any network as well; you may want to change the wording to fit a net work it might read something like this:

We the members of the this network, in Order to survive, form this network, to establish justice, and insure domestic tranquility, provide for the common defence, promote the general welfare, and secure the blessings of liberty to ourselves and our posterity, and to uphold and defend the;

CONSTITUTION of

UNITED STATES of

AMERICA

CHAPTER 10

ENTERTAINMENT

There are many reasons to have as many forms of entertainment as possible one of the most important is boredom, remember idle hand are the devils work shop.

Remember back at the beginning of the book, when I listed people in my network, I said and then there is me, now you can figure out what I meant.

COMPUTER

You mostly will not have internet service, but most new computed have CD or DVD drives, and I will bet you have CDs and DVDs already. With your computer, you can listen to music, watch movies, and even play games. Most people have family pictures and home movies in their computer, I know I do, even now I sometimes look at my old pictures and watch my home movies, and your friends may have some too, they might enjoy sharing them with you and you just might enjoy watching them.

There are tons of educational CDs and DVDs these

could really help you out. Just remember they is not a do all fix all because every situation is and will be different, so they are starting point.

BOOKS

If you enjoy ready books, a most have, you maybe able to trade books with people. I would have a copy of the Bible it will help when you are down, I also suggest getting books on survival and gardening they might come in handy. There is another reason books could come handy, think hygiene.

HAM RADIO

If you have a Ham Radio, you already know the benefits, if you do not have a Ham Radio, try to get one.

You might be able to talk with other people around the world, to get new and information or just talk to other people. A word of caution here a ham Radio single can be tracked so do not stay on for a long period.

SMART PHONES

Most smart phones have games in them and of course

pictures, here another little trick to remember, most smart phone cameras have a zoom feature, and this might help you see or make out something in the distance.

CARDS, GAMES AND PUZZLES

These are something's you may have laying around your home, they are good to keep your mind occupied and to get to know your friends even better.

OUT DOOR GAMES

Look around you home, you may have a basketball, football, baseball and gloves, you may even have
Horse shoes, croquet set, or yard darts basically
anything that can get you out of the house and into the sun, it will do your mind and body good,

BOW AND ARROWS

I may not be a fan of using a bow and arrow for hunt, mainly because you need to practice a lot to learn how to use one good enough to hunt with. You set up some kind of target to shot at, and provide yourself a form of entertainment. You will also be learning how to shoot the bow and arrow, at some point you could use it as a weapon or to hunt with.

When you are outside playing someone needs to be keeping watch and can sound the alarm if someone or something approaches. In addition, someone needs to be on watch 24-7-365. Always remember the quote by Louis Pasteur chance favors only the prepared mind and in the fields of observation this especially true.

Just because you are trying to survive a bad situation does not mean you cannot have some fun.

CHAPTER 11

BUG-IN OR BUG-OUT

LOCATION, LOCATION, LOCATION

Bug out WHY, where are you going to go, how much can you take with you, and who and what are you going to encounter along the way.

Oh that's right, you got a bug out bag, give me a flipping break. I went out and got me a big fat backpack loaded it up with all the stuff the experts recommended I have in it, a three day supply of food, ten pounds, three gallons of water, twenty four pounds, a gun and ammo five pounds, first aid kit, flash light, a tent, radio, extra cloths and don't forget the back pack itself, well folks that is well over fifty (50) pounds.

I consider myself to be in a little better than average physical condition and I really do not think I can walk very far with a fifty (50) pack on and heaven forbid having to run, and I know my wife could not.

I think you get my point, it is called shelter in place.

My location is known only to my network. It may a network member's house or a location elsewhere and most likely more than one location.

My location has been or will selected for the following reasons,

One easy access point (street, road) that can be easily defended and several ways to leave just in case.

It is to be near multiple water sources.

It has more than one source of heat for cooking and purifying water.

It has access to fuel and energy sources natural gas, propane, solar, wind, and wood.

When the gas and propane runs out and unless the sun goes out, I will use solar and wind, I have acres and acres of trees that can cut for fire wood and building.

It has adequate space for a garden one half acre open space with plenty of sun light.

Solid Brick construction with raised crawl space foundation. My crawl space is dry and temperature is far above and below the outside. The crawl space has vents to allow for ventilation they can also be used for gun placements.

It is not a good idea to store anything in an attic in the summer temperatures can exceed 160 degrees, a house with a crawl space foundation is a much better choice, and my house has between 2 and 6 feet of headroom more than enough to store food and water. If I need to, I can cut a hole in my floor to access the crawl space so I will not need to go outside to get food and water.

You must be able to see if anything approaches from any direction. I have clear lines of sight (360)

Throughout time people have been building emplacements to protect themselves and others from hostile invaders more commonly known as a FORT, my fort will protect the network form small groups and small weapons.

If for some strange reason the military came a calling, and I think possibility, that happening is very unlikely, because they will have much bigger problems to deal with than little old me.

However, if it does happen about all I or anyone else could do is run and hide until they leave, then I will return to get the stuff that they did not find, remember the PVC pipe I talked about earlier.

If they do not leave after a short time, I have more one than one backup plan, and locations and well let us just say pit stops along the way.

I do not tell everything to anyone and I have places to go some are as close a one half mile and others as far a 75 miles away.

I know that at some point the network may need to separate in order to survive, sometimes a small group can move faster than a large group, and a small group is harder to find.

Remember to have a plan in place before you need it, know what and how much will be given to each person, this will help prevent problems if the group needs to split up.

Once a friend always a friend and do not forget that. There may come a time when you friends, network, group or whatever you want to call it, may be able too and need to come back together. You have a plan for that, setup a couple of predetermined places that can be check on from time to time. Remember there was a reason you were to together in the first place.

There is strength in numbers.

If you still feel the need to bug out, I suggest you get an older vehicle power by a diesel engine Everybody tells you diesel, however no one tells you why to get a diesel engine, so I reckon I will give you a couple of reasons to get an older diesel power source.

Older diesel engines will run on many different types of. oils, mineral and vegetable oil even used vegetable oil. Older diesel engines do not need electricity to run, they run off of the compression generated.

The power to fuel ratio is much better, this means the engine runs slower with more power and less fuel consumption.

The new diesel engines have so many electronics, the biggest problem is electronic fuel injection and another is an electric fuel pump. Should we experience an electro magnetic pulse they are not going to work.

One of the big problems with diesel engines is, they do not like the cold. You should keep the fuel and engine warm if possible.

Another problem with a diesel engine, is do not let it run out of fuel, if you do you may get air in the fuel lines and filters, if you do, it can be fixed, but it can be a S.O.B. to fix. Been there done that.
I still say bug in and shelter in place.

CHAPTER 12

SECURITY

Yes by now you should know that I am a believer in the second amendment to the US Constitution

A well-regulated Militia, being necessary to the security of a Free State, the right of the people to keep and bear Arms, shall not be infringed.

I also believe that if guns are outlawed only outlaws will have guns.

Since the gun ban fear, gun and ammunition has become harder to find and the prices have in some cases double and quadrupled. Just give it a little while it will come back down.

I have listed a few of my favorites and not so favorites. These are only a few of the hundreds of choice you have, find the ones that are right for you and get properly trained on how to use them.

22 LONG RIFLES

A 22 Rifle is in my opinion the single most import weapon you should have, it can be used for short and medium long range shooting , it is not as loud and can be operated by just about anyone, it has very little recoil (kick) and up until recently the ammunition was inexpensive. You could get it just about anywhere.

22 PISTOLS

A 22 Caliber pistol is small, and easy to carry. Because the ammunition is small and light weight, you can carry a lot of rounds. A 22 dose not have the knock down power of larger weapons, however it will stop most anything thing you may encounter or at least it will think twice about continuing at you.

I want to get a suppressor (silencer) and yes they are legal, however you need to go through the proper steps to get one. I plan to get one that will fit on my 22 rifle and pistol. The paper work and suppressor will cost several hundred dollars.

38 Special

Good personal protection, fair knock down power, most people can handle this pistol. Price of ammo not too bad.

357 MAG.

Better hold on to this bad boy, it kicks like a mule, it will knock most things off its feet and, they probably are not going to get up. Ammo for the 357 mag. a little pricey but it is worth it for the power you get. To save money you can use 38 special rounds in a 357.

9MM

Not one of my personal favorites, less knock down power, but has more penetrating power. Fast bullets used by Military and Law Enforcement. Ammo price wise not too bad. I just prefer more knock power.

40 CAL

I think the 40 caliber is the best of both worlds, Not to much recoil, great knock down power and good penetrating power as well. Still used by many law enforcement officers. The price of ammo for the 40 cal a little more than the 9mm.

45 CAL

A lot people who like the Model 1911 45, It has great knock down power big bullet, easy to handle once you get use to it. The bullet is a slow mover; you can almost see the bullet flying through the air. The 45 used to be the gold standard for the military, until they switch to the 9mm. I cannot figure that one out, but anyway, the price of the ammo is not too bad.

AR-15 223 RIFLES

Well, the AR-15 is the civilian version of the military M16 sort of, the AR is a Semi automatic weapon, it is more of a long range weapon, if you are a real good shot maybe up to a 1000 yards, but for me maybe a couple hundred yards, very fast bullet speed, easy to handle, not a lot of kick, but you still need to hold on to it. Ammo is easy to get and cheap enough that you can take it target shooting, the AR-15 could also be used for hunting, not the best choice for hunting. Next to the

22, it my favorite target shooting gun.

30-06 RIFLE

Ouch, this a long range gun, it kicks like a mule, and will knock one down as well. Great gun for hunting big game, like deer, hogs, and even bigger game. Ammo is a little pricey.

SHOTGUN

12 GAUGE PUMP

The Vice President is right everybody should get a 12 gauge shotgun, they are great for hunting and home protection, it a close range gun, and at close range will stop almost everything. I like #4 shot or bigger, it is big enough to get your point across. Buckshot will tear things apart, buckshot will blow a big hole in most doors, that alone will make a bad guy think twice about coming in uninvited. If you want to shot larger game like deer I suggest using slugs, just keep in mind a 12 gauge shotgun is a close range gun. You should know a 12 gauge has a lot of recoil or kick so brace yourself. Shells for a 12-gauge shotgun are normally priced good. I bought a case of 250 # 4 shot for around $65.

SHOTGUN 20 GAUGE PUMP

This is a woman's or youth's gun, STOP right there before you get your panties in a wad. I know there are some ladies that can handle larger weapons and are even better shots than I am, some can most likely whip my butt in a fight.

I have no problem having a woman on my team or even being on woman's team. I was raised to respect women, I was also raised to protect and provide for them, and if you have a problem with that, you need to get over it or you do not need to be in my group.

A 20-gauge shotgun is a light gun, and does not have as much recoil as the 12 gauge; it is a great at close range point and shoot from the hip gun. The 20 gauge is a better choice for people of smaller statue and those who are not familiar with shooting. The ammo is easy to find and is not that expensive about the same as a 12 gauge.

I like Mossberg pump shotguns, well-built, solid gun,

easy to maintain and are reasonably priced.

Another reason I like a pump shotgun is when you pump or rack a shell in the chamber, the sound it makes will make most people think twice about advancing toward you, you might could say that sound is your warning shot. A shotgun at close range makes big holes in things.

BOW and ARROWS

I am sorry but a bow and arrow is not a great choice for hunting, unless you have time to do a lot practicing, it is a very close range weapon, the arrows are expensive, break easily and are hard to find when you miss. The only good thing about a bow is it is silent.

CROSSBOW

A crossbow is a good choice for hunting and for defense, it is like some farts silent but deadly. The hard part about using a crossbow is cocking it, if you can get one with a cocker and at least 150 lbs of draw, if you can get close enough you can drop a deer, just remember it is still a close range weapon. The bolts are not cheap so be sure to hit what you are shooting at. Shoot it like you would shoot a rifle.

CROSSBOW PISTOL

I bought a crossbow pistol think it would be a fun little toy to shoot at cardboard targets.

How dumb am I, IT IS NOT A TOY, it can be a deadly weapon. The one I have will propel the 6-inch bolt through a one half inch thick piece of plywood that is more than enough power to kill small game and even people at close range.

The one I have also has a built in cocker, safety, and cost less the 50 dollars.

STUN GUN

If for some unknown reason you allow someone to get up close a personal a stun gun, will in most cases get him or her off you and incapacitate that person long enough for you to get away. I know you have heard this before (don't try this at home), take my word for it don't try this at home and do not test a stun gun on your friends either.

BLADES

Knifes, you can not have too many, long ones, short one, flat point, sharp point, fixed blade or folding blades, you need them all. One my favorites is an assist open (switchblade) made by Kershaw, and as strange as it may sound it is legal to own and carry in most places. The nice thing about an assist open knife, is it does not take both hands to open or close.

The next knife you should have is a survival type knife the ones with a hollow handle with a screw on cape. Most of these type of survival knifes come with some items that are handy if you get in a tight spot, like fishing line and hooks, matches and striker and a compass or you can build your kit to put in the handle.

It does not matter if it is cheap or expensive, I would buy one that did not have a saw back blade, and it is good for sawing small wood and bones. I have several some cost as little as $10 and some well cost a lot more.

I like swords, my favorite is a Samurai Katana. This sword is longer, which allows for a little more distance between you and an a attacker. The ones with stainless steel blades are in most cases stronger and can take more abuse they are harder to sharpen when they get dull. I prefer a high carbon steel blade, even thou it will not take as much abuse and it will rust, it is much easier to sharpen, and it honed to a near razors edge.

I also prefer the handle to be leather and cord wrapped; it is much easier to hold on to if your hands get wet either way, a sword is not meant to chop wood. If you need to do chop wood, get a machete or hatchet.

MACHETE

The machete is frequently used to cut undergrowth and cutting limbs off trees. You can use it for such household tasks as cutting large food, splitting kindling, yard work, and clearing brush. The machete can also be used as a weapon kinda like a sword. The machete is a must have tool.

SPEARS

A spear does not need to fancy, you can make a spear out of just about anything, a broom handle, a limb from a tree or a piece of PVC pipe. Make sure it is ridged and as straight so it does not wobble when you throw it. A spear can be used in many ways, you can throw it, swing it, use it to poke and jab with it, you can place one end on the ground, put your foot on it to anchor it to the ground hold at 45 degree angle to prevent someone or something from charging you. Whatever you use just put a sharp point on it.

DUST MASK

Have you ever been the south in the springtime of the year, the pollen is so bad; sometimes it looks like green clouds blowing in the wind. The pollen gets on and in everything. A cheap dust mask can help us people who suffer from allergies.

A dust mask can also help prevent you from getting sick, if you have to be around someone who is sick.

They may offer a little protection from other things, but I will not bet my life on it. Dust mask are so cheap, that everyone should have dozens and dozens of them. I bought a dozen for less than five dollars. Of course, some are much more expensive.

GAS MASK

My first question is, why do you think you need a gas mask. If it is for a threat that you can see coming, like someone shooting tear gas at you or in your house, a gas mask will help. But for the bad boys like anthrax, nuclear, and the other stuff that can really kill you, you will most likely not see it coming and by the time you realize it   is too late to put on a gas mask.

Unless if you have an early warning system you are screwed, blued and tattooed and a gas mask will not help you

If you still feel you want or need a gas mask I would

suggest you get a gas masks uses the standard NATO 40mm threaded gas filters (DO NOT get one that uses proprietary filters).

The filter on the gas is the most important thing get a filter that has a NBC rating (Nuclear, Biological and Chemical) a NBC filter a CBA/RCA (Chemical Blowing and Riot Control Agent) rating as well. I do not suggest getting a specialty filters used for specific agents.

Many people ask how long the filters last; the best answer I have found so far is a conservative number of eight (8) hours.

However, the time varies greatly depending on the gas and concentrations and your breathing rate. It is like scuba diving the faster you breather the more air you use, a gas mask has a limited amount of filter space, so the faster you breathe means you will bring more stuff into the filter faster, clogging it up faster.

The time a filter last is not the most important thing. What is important is that your mask last long enough for you to get out of the threatened area. You may be able to extend the effective of the filter by wrapping it with a dust mask or even a coffee filter.

Ok so you still want to get a gas mask I suggest you get a full-face mask with eye lenses and even better get a head and shoulder hood. I think our military uses this type gas mask now that should tell you something.

A full body suit is the best of the best; it will protect your whole body.

Let us say you were lucky enough to get your gas mask or suit on in time and make to your house, you walk in the door, and you have just contaminated your house, everybody, and everything in it. When you take, your protective gear off you just contaminated yourself.

The way to prevent contamination is simple, take a shower outside of your house using a biological soap. If you can rigged up a ventilation system, which pulls filtered air in to the shower, and vent it out of the shower that is even better.

Now that I have scared the bjusses out of you, I am buying a couple of NBC gas mask with extra filters. Hey, you cannot be too careful.

AIR FILTERS

Ok you made it back to your house, got all cleaned up, did you think about an air filtration for you house. I mean get real people, how smart would it be to make it back to your house just to die when you get there.

PERISCOPE

It is better to look around or over things using a periscope than sticking your head up and getting shot. Periscopes are not very expensive.

BINOCULARS

All the better to see you with. I have both large ones and small ones, the large ones I can use at my base station and the small ones I will carry with me when I go out searching for things.

NIGHT VISION BINOCULARS and SCOPES

The price of night vision scopes and binoculars have

come way down in the last few year. You can spend anywhere from $150 to up into the thousands.

I will buy the lower end; I am not planning on being a sniper, but you never know.

VIDEO CAM

I have an old one that I have not used in years. I dug it out of the closet and it still works, the reason I suggest you have one is the digital zoom.   I have one that has a 2000x zoom. Great for extra long-range viewing.

SURVEILLANCE CAMERAS

I have, well just say a cheap set, two cameras, and receiver that connect to a computer or TV. The cameras have an infrared feature for viewing at night. Being able to see at night is a good thing.

BOOBY-TRAPS

When I say booby traps I am talking about thing you can place around the perimeter of you property something that when tripped will make noise to alert you that something has entered your safe zone.

GET REAL PEOPLE

I found some exploding booby traps on BUDK's website. They a basically a firecracker tied between to pieces of string, if you tie them between two trees, when something trips them it sounds like a firecracker going off. They are very cheap.

Another good way to make booby traps is to tie some cans with rocks in them, again when someone trips thing they will make noise.

Anything you can setup that will alert you when someone or something enters your safe zoon hopefully will give you enough time to react before it get too close.

ELECTRIC FENCE CHARGER AND WIRE

You can buy a solar powered electric fence charge, that works pretty good, the wire in fairly inexpensive, run the wire around the premaster of your property, trust me if some one runs into it you will know. A word of advice do not forget where the wire is and do not take a leak on the wire, it is funny when someone else does it however it will not be funny if you do it. Yep you guessed it.

CANNON

The kind of cannon I am talking about here is made using PVC pipe, it is more for making a big bang than shooting things, however they do not need to know that. It is kind of like a potato gun and yes it can shoot small things, if you are going to build one use at least a schedule 40 PVC pipe the heavier the better.

I feel sure if you think about it you can think of other thing as well.

There has been so much talk about high capacity magazines, mostly by people who really do not have a clue.

It does not matter how many round you have in a magazine, someone who knows how to use a weapon knows how to change an empty magazines out, with a full one faster than you can get to them.

The reason I like high capacity magazines is simple, when I am in my TARGET shooting stance, I can stay on target longer. It is also a lot safer, the less time you spend fiddling with the weapon, the less time there is for accidents, and yes there is always a chance for an accident even to the most carful people in the world.

I would like you to stop and think about this, would you attack a person, holding a four feet long sword, do you know how much damage an idiot with a sword can do in a crowd.

There are very few of us that are brave enough to try to stop a person with a sword. So I recon the next thing they will want to ban will be swords

CHAPTER 13

GET OR GIVE HELP

Let me start off by saying I will give you the shirt off my back if you ask, but you try to steal from me I will shoot you dead and then take what you have, and will not lose a minutes sleep when I do. So you have been warned.

If you come to me in need, if I can I will help you, but I will ask you to earn it, I might need help cutting wood, hauling water, harvesting food.

There is no free ride, I am not the government, and I am not the welfare office, I do not give food stamps, you should have thought of this.

I have worked hard for everything I have, I do not have much, but I earned it from hard work and planning.

Remember this

"A prudent man foresees the difficulties ahead and prepares for them; the simpleton goes blindly on and suffers the consequences." -

Proverbs 22:3

Yes, I know I have said this before, you can not in your wildest dream know how important those sayings are. If you forget them you may not survive.

CHAPTER 14

WEBSITES

Below are some websites that I like. Some of the things I have talked about or referred to can be found on the following websites. There are thousands maybe millions of website that offer survival gear and helpful and not so helpful information.

I take everything with a grain of salt, until I have used it or researched it until I am comfortable buying it or using it.

Tip # One. If you see something on a website, see how many other websites offer the same product.

Tip # Two read the customers reviews, but DO NOT read the reviews on the products website, (do you think the company is really going to post real reviews) go to a website like Amazon or Wal-Mart the reviews are most likely truer because those site would not have to deal with the returns because of a fake review. Unfortunately there are no grantees some bad products will not get a good review. Just remember if it sounds too good to be true it probably is too good to be true. I do not indorse any product.

Tip # Three. Many sites have the user manuals online read the manual before you buy the product, if you can not understand the manual, the product may be difficult to use and maintain.

WATER

Berkey Water Filter

I have seen it in action, and I like it

http://www.berkeyfilters.com

Well Water Boy

They make a bucket to draw water from wells

Just tie a rope to the bucket, lower it into, it fills with water, then just pull it back out and you have a couple of gallons of water.

http://www.wellwaterboy.com/catalog/c5_p1.html

POWER

Northern tool has so many things I want and I have

bought many different things from and will buy more.
http://www.northerntool.com/

http://www.northerntool.com/shop/tools/product_200595038_200595038

http://www.northerntool.com/shop/tools/product_200439926_200439926

http://www.northerntool.com/shop/tools/category_alternative-renewable-energy+dc-powered-refrigerators-freezers.

Adapter to make tri-fuel generator http://uscarb.com
BioLite Stoves
http://www.biolitestove.com

SECURITY

CHEAPER THAN DIRT
I have bought from and will buy more from Cheaper than Dirt
http://www.cheaperthandirt.com/

CABELAS

You may want to check Cables out; I have bought a bunch of stuff and will buy more.

http://www.cabelas.com

BUDK

Not everything is name brand but BUDK's has some cool things that you cannot find at other place, I like it

http://www.budk.com

FOOD

I have tried a few of the prepackaged dried food products from these place, well the food is not as good as momma makes but if you are trying to survive the are pretty darn good if you juice them up with the herbs and spices that hopefully you stocked up on.

They are a little on the expensive side, but remember they are doing all the work, cooking, drying and packaging and there is a lot to be said for that.

I am looking at a kit that will feed 4 people for one year, which should feed two people for two years and when I combine that kit with my other food, I will do more than just survive until I get my garden in and harvested. I will eat well. http://wisefoodstorage.com/

http://www.mountainhouse.com/

http://www.augasonfarms.com/

PLEASANT HILL GRAIN
http://www.pleasanthillgrain.com

Nesco/American Harvest
Dehydrator, bought one, I use it a lot, and I love it, enough said
http://www.nesco.com

I am list a few website that offer a lot of different things from food to storage containers and everything in between

EMERGENCY ESSENTIALS http://beprepared.com
LEXINGTON CONTAINER COMPANY
http://www.lexingtoncontainercompany.com

AUSTIN AIR

http://austinair.com/

AMAZON

http://www.amazon.com

SURVIVAL WAREHOUSE

http://www.survival-warehouse.com

If you are wondering why I am listing websites, it real simple, right now the internet is on, if something happens there will not be an internet and even if there is you will not be able to order any thing.

I know I sound like a broken record, but the point I am trying to make is, make a plan and work the plan now. If you wait until something happens it will be too late and it will be your own fault.

CHAPTER 15

THE HARD DECISIONS

There may come a time when you will need to make some very hard decisions. The decisions will affect you and your friends for the rest of your life.

I hope you will never be put in a life or death situation, but if you are, you can not over think you must react, if you do not, it can cost you and your friends their lives. As much as I would hate to take the life of anyone, I can tell you I will if anyone tries to hurt my family and friends.

When people go to the grocery store and find there is no food on the shelves or turn on the faucet and the water does not come out water you can bet that panic will set in, after they realize what has happened their survival instinct will kick in you had better be prepared because they are not your friends anymore.

I do not want to say they are your enemies however if they find out you have food and water and because they did not prepare they are going to want you to give them your food and water, the same food and water that you worked very hard storing for weeks, months and maybe years, while they sat on their rear end doing nothing and in some cases laughing at you and calling you crazy just because you were trying to prepare for what if.

Then they will be like cats, if you feed them once they will not leave. If you stop helping them then they will try to take what you have. Do not think bad of them they are just trying to survive just like you are, the difference is they did not prepare.

The next problem you have is that if you give them a little food and water and they do leave they will be back and may bring friends with them. If you turn them away without anything they will of course they will be upset, they could meet up with someone else, tell them they know where there is food and water, but the people there will not help anyone out, now you don't have one person to worry about you have two and maybe more.

I would most likely give them a little some thing, and tell them if I see them, again, I will shoot them on sight and I will be prepared to do so.

If they have something to trade, I will see if they have something I need or could use, that is different they help me I will help them.

Another problem that may occur is someone in your group decides to leave, I would give them a pack of supplies so they could survive for maybe a week, but they will need to know once they leave there is no coming back.

When you abandoned your house, guess what, most people are just going to grab what they can carry, and leave all sorts of things. Things I can use like food maybe guns and ammo and I bet you have a propane grill which means you have a propane tank with propane in it, well it is mine now.

I may leave you a note with my phone number on it so you can call me if you come back, oops, I forgot there is no phone service, sorry about that. I am not trying to be funny, but I think you now understand, that if I could ask you for something I would but I cannot ask you so I will just take it, and I guess that is stealing.

On the flip side if I find your car or come to your house and you are there I will swap some of what I have for what you have and knowing me I would try to help you out even if you do not have anything to trade.

People the best tool and weapon you have is your mind. Look around and survey your surroundings, take inventory of what you have, you will be surprised what you have.

Now is the time to add to your supplies, when you go to the store, do not buy just one of something buy two, the impact on your budget will be small, the impact on your survival will be huge.

Something else I figured out is buying in bulk can save you money in the long run.

Remember, I said I bought fifty pounds of rice for less than twenty dollars.

If you go to your local feed store you can buy fifty pounds of shelled corn for around eleven dollars.

Remember to keep your grains in an air tight container, in a cool dry place, this will help keep moisture and bugs out.

You may think I am preparing for world war three, but I am not, I am preparing for what ever may occur. I have seen the storms that cause power outages, that in some case last for weeks. I have seen the financial market almost collapse.

What I now realize is that I can not depend on the government to come to the rescue because the government is what has caused most the problems to start with.

When half of the people are being supported by the other half of the people that is a real problem.

I do want to make it very, very clear, I am not talking about the people who have work all their lives and pay into the social security system or our military who have made this country the greatest country on earth and who have made it possible for me to have what I have and do what I do.

The people I am talking about are the ones who can but do not work, they have figured out that they can get ever thing for free from the government, some of them live better than I do. Those people have not earned the right to survive.

To those people I give this warning, I am not the government and I will not give your lazy, good for nothing butt anything and you have nothing I need or want.

If you see something like this as you approach my house,

You should realize you are in a kill zone, and turn around run away as fast as you, don't worry I will not shoot you in the back, so consider it your only warning shot. I do not shoot to wound, I shoot to kill.

With the above said, if your intent is to trade something you may have and if I can use it or need it and I have something you may need and I can spare, by all means we will talk, you can not ever tell we might even get a long term swap meet going.

Just be sure to let me know what is on your mind before you approach.

God help you if you try to take from me, my family and friends. These are the only people that have earned the right to survive.

It is a bad situation but if it is going to happen, you need to prepare yourself.

Now that you have finished reading my short little book, you probable think I have thousands of gallons of water and hundred and hundreds of pounds of food, maybe tens of thousands of rounds of ammo. Well you would be wrong.

Things I have for the most part are thing I have collect over many years, working different jobs. I am somewhat of a packrat. I never wanted to throw anything away because I might need it at some point in the future

My weapons are from hunting and target shooting not because I am worried about doomsday.

The water containers I needed to water trees we planted and there was not anywhere close enough the access a water supply.

I buy bulk food and supplies because they are cheaper and I like to save money. We eat a fair amount of rice, rice will keep a long time, and a fifty pound bag of anything is cheaper per pound than buying a small bag or box.

Ever since I was ten years old, my family has had some

sort of wood burning stove or fireplace, which explains why I have axes, splitters, and all kinds of saws.

Ok now you know that I am a tight wad and like the way some things were done as they say in the old days.

So you see I am not prepping for doomsday, I really don't think it is going to happen in my life time.

What all this talk has done is make me aware of my surroundings. It has also made me aware of how much I had been wasting and all of the things I have that can be used just in case.

I am going not to change the way I live. If you came buy my house you would be disappointed at how unprepared it looks, but that is the point, Hide in plain sight. Remember do not judge a book by its cover.

I can only hope, something in the book helps someone in some small way.

There is so much more I will be writing about in the future, so be on the look out.

See ya, on the flip side or maybe not